D0126148

WHY ARE SOME
BEACHES OILY?

BY ISAAC ASIMOV

ASHE COUNTY PUBLIC LIBRARY
Rt. 1, Library Drive
West Jefferson, NC 28694-9793

Gareth Stevens Publishing
MILWAUKEE

J363.73
ASI

0102?3946

For a free color catalog describing Gareth Stevens' list of high-quality books, call 1-800-341-3569 (USA) or 1-800-461-9120 (Canada).

Library of Congress Cataloging-in-Publication Data

Asimov, Isaac, 1920-
    Why are some beaches oily? / by Isaac Asimov.
       p. cm. -- (Ask Isaac Asimov)
   Includes bibliographical references and index.
   Summary: Discusses the causes and damaging
effects of oil spills and ways to protect the land and
sea from oil pollution.
   ISBN 0-8368-0796-0
   1. Oil spills--Environmental aspects--Juvenile literature.
2. Oil pollution of water--Environmental aspects--Juvenile
literature. 3. Oil pollution of soils--Environmental aspects--
Juvenile literature. [1. Oil spills. 2. Oil pollution of the sea.
3. Oil pollution of soils. 4. Pollution.] I. Title. II. Series:
Asimov, Isaac, 1920- Ask Isaac Asimov.
TD427.P4A84   1992
363.73'82--dc20   92-5345

Edited, designed, and produced by
Gareth Stevens Publishing
1555 North RiverCenter Drive, Suite 201
Milwaukee, Wisconsin 53212, USA

Text © 1992 by Nightfall, Inc., and Martin H. Greenberg
End matter © 1992 by Gareth Stevens, Inc.
Format © 1992 by Gareth Stevens, Inc.

First published in the United States and Canada by Gareth Stevens, Inc. All rights reserved. No part of this book may be reproduced or used in any form or by any means without permission in writing from Gareth Stevens, Inc.

Picture Credits
pp. 2-3, Kurt Carloni/Artisan, 1992; pp. 4-5, © Malcolm Penny/Survival Anglia; pp. 6-7, Kurt Carloni/Artisan, 1992; p. 7 (inset), Kurt Carloni/Artisan, 1992; pp. 8-9, © James Willis/IMPACT Photos; pp. 10-11, © Tony Dawson; pp. 12-13, © Greenpeace/Vaccari; pp. 14-15, © Tony Dawson; pp. 16-17, © Tony and Liz Bomford/Survival Anglia; p. 17 (inset), © Greenpeace/Merjenburgh; pp. 18-19, © Greenpeace/Merjenburgh; pp. 20-21, © Jeff Foott/Survival Anglia; pp. 22-23, © Picture Perfect USA, Inc.; p. 24, © Picture Perfect USA, Inc.

Cover photograph, © Greenpeace/Grace: A gentoo penguin examines its oil-soaked wings. Oil spills can damage and destroy all kinds of marine wildlife.

Series editor: Elizabeth Kaplan
Editor: Valerie Weber
Series designer: Sabine Beaupré
Picture researcher: Diane Laska

Printed in MEXICO

1 2 3 4 5 6 7 8 9 98 97 96 95 94 93 92